Piccolo
A Piper Book

Contents

MUSIC

By
David Moses

Editor: Deri Warren

Piccolo
A Piper Book

Music Today

Musicians are among the best-known people in the world today, often more famous than sportsmen, politicians or even royalty. Many rock stars have been forced to sneak away from concerts using side entrances, to avoid being set upon by over-eager fans, while some orchestral players and composers are so familiar to the general public that their faces and voices have been used to advertise products connected with music. Members of pop groups from places such as Sweden and Jamaica have been recognized as stars in almost every country in the world.

A hundred years ago, this kind of fame would only have been possible for a few concert soloists or opera singers, and their audiences would have been confined to the wealthy and privileged. The majority of people would scarcely have been aware of their existence. A hundred years before that, the musician who managed to become a professor of music, a choir master or a court musician in the house of a wealthy nobleman would have considered himself to have been successful and fortunate.

Musicians owe this change in their fortunes to three quite recent inventions — the gramophone, radio and television.

Birth of an Industry

The gramophone was invented in 1877 by Thomas Alva Edison. Edison himself became the world's first recording artist, with his recitation of 'Mary had a little lamb'.

Unlike today's sophisticated electronics, Edison's first recording was a purely mechanical process. He spoke into a mouthpiece containing a thin disc of iron, called a diaphragm, which was fixed to a needle. The sound of his voice made the diaphragm vibrate, and the moving needle scratched a pattern of grooves onto a cylinder covered in tin foil.

The recording was played back through a lighter diaphragm made of parchment, which was attached to a steel stylus. As the handle connected to the cylinder was turned, the grooves on the cylinder moved the stylus up and down. This caused the parchment diaphragm to vibrate, producing sound.

By the 1920s, the diaphragm had been replaced by a microphone which changed the voice vibrations into an electric signal. This signal caused the needle to vibrate as it cut a groove into the record. The cylinder had also been replaced, by a flat disc made out of a brittle substance called shellac.

These early recordings were very tricky and expensive. The artist had only one chance to get the performance right, and if there were any mistakes the disc was

Left: Before popular songs became available on record, people bought sheet music so that they could play them at home.

Thomas Edison

ruined. However, the invention of the tape recorder, first used commercially in the 1940's, made it possible to record several 'takes' of the same piece and then transfer the best onto disc.

Guglielmo Marconi

Radio and Television

Although Guglielmo Marconi sent the first radio signals through the air in the 1890s, it was not until the 1920s that radio began to be used for entertainment.

John Logie Baird

Radio was soon followed by the development of television by John Logie Baird. The first TV service was broadcast by the BBC in 1936, and by the 1950s televised concerts were being seen and heard by audiences all over the world.

Recording Today

Perhaps the most important recent development in recording has been multi-tracking. This allows a musician to record a performance and then, while replaying the tape, to add extra instruments or voices.

Modern studios have machines which can record up to 64 tracks. This means that each voice and instrument in a group can be recorded onto a separate track. When the tape is played back, each track can be

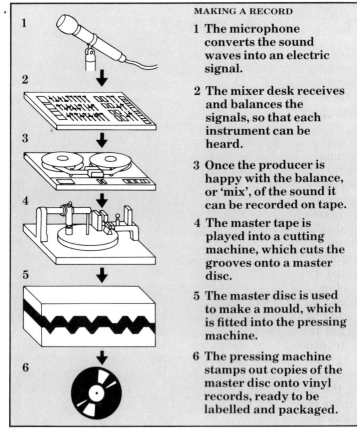

MAKING A RECORD

1 **The microphone converts the sound waves into an electric signal.**

2 **The mixer desk receives and balances the signals, so that each instrument can be heard.**

3 **Once the producer is happy with the balance, or 'mix', of the sound it can be recorded on tape.**

4 **The master tape is played into a cutting machine, which cuts the grooves onto a master disc.**

5 **The master disc is used to make a mould, which is fitted into the pressing machine.**

6 **The pressing machine stamps out copies of the master disc onto vinyl records, ready to be labelled and packaged.**

made louder or softer, or treated with echo and other electronic effects.

Above: A modern recording studio.

Once the musicians or their producer decide there is no more to be added or removed, the whole lot can be 'mixed' back down to two tracks to make a stereo tape recording ready for cutting onto disc.

However, even the best quality magnetic tape produces a 'hiss', and very slightly distorts the true sound. Because of this, some studios are now recording music onto a computer instead of a tape recorder. The signal from the microphone is translated into computer language, and the computer then sends this information to the tool which cuts the groove on the disc. This produces a 'master' disc which is used to make a metal mould. Copies of the disc are then stamped out by the mould.

Musical Superstars

It was only when radio sets became cheap enough for most people to own that recording artists could hope for international fame. The result of hearing more music on the radio was that more and more people bought gramophone records. During the early days of recording, to sell a thousand copies of a record must have been quite exceptional. Today, sales of over a million copies are not uncommon, and record companies spend enormous sums of money on recording and promoting their stars.

Music All Around

The words 'fame' and 'star' are frequently used when talking about music and musicians. These words suggest a type of music which is widely admired and played for the purpose of our amusement and enjoyment.

However, not all music is intended to be listened to, at least not consciously. Taped background music is played in airliners, supermarkets and hotels, for example, in order to make people feel relaxed and comfortably at

Below: Horror films rely on music to 'set the scene'.

home. Music is used in drama as a form of extra scenery. In cinema, television and radio, moods of calmness, tension, pathos and humour can often be created more effectively through music than with words or pictures. Try comparing the effect of watching a horror film on TV with the sound turned up and then down. You will find that the music of the soundtrack tells you how to react, and what to expect next.

On a more serious level, some music, like a great poem or painting, may cause you to marvel at the genius of the composer, or be moved

Above: During World War II, patriotic popular music was used to keep the troops' spirits up.

by the images of beauty, tragedy or grandeur it conjures up. Great church music has been written to celebrate people's religious beliefs, while military music is intended to stir the heart and fill the mind with brave and patriotic thoughts.

Throughout the ages, composers have been called on to fill a great variety of musical needs, and the purposes for which music has been intended has shaped its growth and development.

13

Right: A cave painting showing a hunter dressed in a bison's skin. The instrument he is playing would have probably made a noise like the bellow of his prey.

Below: Music probably began with the magical rites of the cave dwellers.

How Music Began

Strange though it may seem, primitive people may have invented musical instruments long before the idea of making music was born.

Our early ancestors had to survive in a wild and hostile world, where unexpected and terrifying things seemed to happen as if by magic. Only by possessing a more powerful magic could they hope to keep one step ahead of disaster.

Anyone who could use an instrument to produce a noise like a demon wailing, a bull roaring, a rattlesnake, a bird — or better still, like nothing on Earth — was thought to possess magical powers. For example, talking through a large sea shell made a voice sound hollow and mysterious, while blowing down it made an even weirder noise. A hollow reed could produce a soft, haunting warble or a wild scream, while the twang from a hunter's bow could be made louder by resting one end against the hunter's open mouth.

Early Civilizations

Our first real evidence of musical activity was provided by the first civilizations, which had grown up from the earliest farming settlements.

The First Farmers

In time, early people began to realize that herding animals offered an easier lifestyle than hunting them. They left their caves and built huts and villages, and planted crops for themselves and their animals. The villages grew into towns, and the first civilizations began.

As people learnt new skills, their problems of survival altered. They could still be destroyed by powers beyond their control, but somehow flooding and drought seemed more remote than being trodden on by a mammoth. The role of music reflected this new way of life.

Mesopotamia

Today, the rivers Tigris and Euphrates flow across the dry and rocky country of Iraq. But 6000 years ago, the land of Mesopotamia which

**Below:
Mesopotamian
musicians.**

lay between the rivers was so fertile that there was no need for everyone to grow crops or herd animals.

Some people became craftsmen, making utensils, ornaments and weapons. Others became chiefs or law makers, soldiers or priests — and some became musicians.

In the great city temples, priests would try to please the terrible gods of famine, fire, flood or thunder. Music played an important part in the temple ceremonies. Each god was thought to have a favourite instrument, such as reed flutes, oboes, harps or goblet-shaped drums.

Egypt

The earliest Egyptian civilization was similar to that of the Mesopotamians. Historians know little about the type of music played in this period except that it was quiet, restrained and slow-moving by modern standards. Wall paintings show dancers and musicians in calm, graceful attitudes, and they are shown playing small flutes and harps — instruments often associated with peace and meditation. The shape of the harps, however, clearly reflects a link with the bows of the hunters.

Above: Egyptian wall painting showing female harpist.

In the fields and vineyards, flat sticks were clapped together to scare off birds and other pests. When calling on their gods to make the crops grow, the Egyptians used these same sticks to provide a **rhythm** for dancing. In another ceremony, a priestess carried a sistrum (bells attached to a Y-shaped frame), as a sign of divine power. Other musicians played a 'double clarinet', and kept air in their cheeks to allow them to keep blowing through the instrument while breathing in at the same time.

17

Arab and Asian Influences

As more civilizations grew up they began to trade with one another. Musicians often travelled with the merchants, and so music from one area spread to another. National styles of music also underwent a change when countries invaded one another.

Usually, the music of the conquerors replaced or altered that of the invaded country. However, when Egyptian armies conquered parts of Asia and what is now the Arab world, Egyptian music was swamped by new and exciting sounds. Dancing girls swirled to loud drums and cymbals, wild oboes and shrill flutes, harps and passionate lutes.

China

Meanwhile, in China, musical traditions had been formed before Egyptian times. According to legend, in around 2700 BC a Chinese emperor decreed that the sound of a particular 'yellow bell' should form the basis of Chinese music. Since then, the style of the music has changed very little over thousands of years. Traditional instruments, such as stone or bell chimes, globular

Above: The wild Arabic music swept the Egyptians off their feet.

flutes, a mouth organ shaped like a cup full of celery sticks, zithers and something very like a banjo are still used in China, Japan and South East Asia today.

Ancient Greece

In ancient Greece, as in China, music was almost regarded as a science, rather than as an art. The rules governing the formation of music and harmony were seen as a pattern that could also be used for running the state and one's personal life.

The main purpose of music was to educate. At one time,

a law was passed that all children living in the area of Sparta should be taught music in order to make them law-abiding citizens. And if a person was considered to be particularly cultivated, the word used to describe them was 'musical'.

The ancient Greeks believed they had two souls — one which desired beauty, order and harmony, and another which yearned for wildness and passion. The god Apollo represented one soul, and Dionysius the other. All serious music was composed in honour of one of these gods. Songs dedicated to Apollo were solemn, and were accompanied on the harp-like lyre. An instrument called an aulos, consisting of two very loud oboe-like instruments joined together, was played in honour of Dionysius.

In the open-air theatres, music and dance played an important part in the tragedies and comedies dedicated to the gods. We can find the seeds of both opera and ballet in ancient Greek drama. When the Greek civilization began to decline, however, drama became merely a show for entertainment, with popular music and circus acts. These were called 'pantomimes'.

Below: The kithara was the lyre played by professional Greek musicians.

19

Ancient Greek music was linked closely to poetry, since music without words was thought by many to be quite meaningless. There were two main types of poetry: epic poetry, which told stories of the gods and heroes, and lyric poetry, which took popular life, love, war and politics as its themes.

Originally, the Olympic Games included contests in music and poetry as well as athletics. In 586 BC, the aulos player Sakadas caused quite a stir by the performance of a purely instrumental piece which described, through music, a fight between Apollo and a dragon.

By this time, the role of Greek music had begun to change. **Virtuoso** (highly skilled) musicians were starting to impose their individuality on music, and were trying to make their instruments more versatile.

Below: The music played on the aulos was fast, rhythmic and exciting.

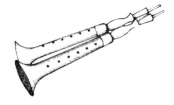

Lyras and Kitharas

As a child, according to Greek legend, the god Hermes killed a turtle. When the shell was empty, he stretched across it the entrails of an ox he had stolen from his brother, Apollo. Then, having invented the lyre, Hermes presented it to Apollo so that he would forgive him for stealing the ox.

The 'lyra', played by amateurs and beginners, was often made from a turtle shell. Professional players used a larger, more strongly-constructed lyre called a 'kithara'. This may well be where the word 'guitar' comes from.

The Hebrews

At one time, the Hebrews wandered the desert as nomads. Abraham led them from Mesopotamia to Palestine in around 2000 BC, and from there they travelled to Egypt in search of grazing pasture. Later, when Moses freed them from Egyptian slavery, they slowly migrated north again.

During their wanderings the Hebrews adopted instruments from other lands as their own. Among these were reed flutes, double oboes (like the Greek aulos),

drums, cymbals, harps and lyres (which they called 'kinnors').

Normally, the Hebrews used the kinnor to accompany bright and lively songs, so when they were forced into exile once again, in Babylon, they wrote 'How can we sing the Lord's song in a strange land?', and left their lyres behind.

Up until this time, no professional musicians had been involved in Jewish religious ceremonies. Although music was important to the ceremonies, it also played such an essential part in everyday life that almost everybody could sing or play an instrument. However, after their return from exile, Israel became a kingdom and professional musicians began to be employed in the Temple built by King Solomon.

Above: Musicians at the Hebrew court.

Trumpets made of rams' horns (called shofa) and of silver (hasosra) were used in religious ceremonies and on special occasions. It is said that these were the trumpets used to blow down the walls of Jericho.

The most important aspect of Jewish religious music was the singing, especially of the Psalms. Like ancient Greek music, the rhythm was governed by the rhythm of the poetry. The Levites (the professional musicians) would sing part of each verse, leaving the congregation to answer. This singing style was adopted by the early Christians, and so helped to shape music throughout the Western world.

Discovering the Past

Our knowledge of the musical life of ancient civilizations has benefited greatly from such archaeological finds as the wall painting shown on the right. The scene, which shows the daughter of a prosperous Roman family learning to play the kithara, tells us as much about the social role of music in ancient Rome as it does about the instrument itself. Myths and legends provide us with further clues, and anthropologists can go back even further by studying rocks and fossils to build up a picture of how primitive people used to live.

In more recent times, accounts left by the wealthy tell us when, where and why various musicians were hired. Poets and writers have left us their impressions of the music they knew, while musicians have always proved to be popular with painters and sculptors.

Musical Detectives

It was not until the Middle Ages that people began to write music down in a way we can recognize today.

Above: A music lesson in ancient Rome. (Wall painting found in Herculaneum, dating from the 1st century AD).

However, the musical language, or **notation,** that musicians use nowadays was invented less than 300 years ago. If we want to read the music written before that time, we have to use the techniques of an historical detective.

Musical language has altered in much the same way as ordinary language. In the 16th century, William Shakespeare wrote 'Awakt shee is shee opes her eie'.

Here the meaning is reasonably clear — 'she has woken up and opened her eyes.'

Some 200 years earlier, Chaucer had written 'A poure widwe was whilom dwelling in a narwe cottage'. It is harder to recognize this kind of English, and rather more detective work is needed to understand this as 'A poor widow once lived in a tiny cottage.' Music historians are faced with similar problems in translating medieval notation.

This early music, which provides us with such an important key to the past, was only written down by medieval scholars. The music of ordinary people was handed down over the generations by ear, often changing as it went.

Below: Folk instruments like the ones shown here have changed very little since ancient times.

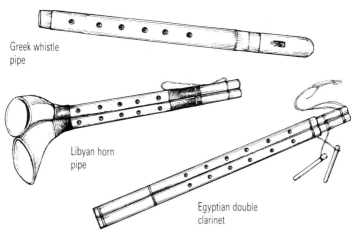

Greek whistle pipe

Libyan horn pipe

Egyptian double clarinet

vuy angıs ꞏ ꞏ uarıes patru uɾao ın uı apl ıuas dc cıo ɾ ꞇ cıa ꝟ
uarıes ꞇ ꝗaleaꝑt uoc eı ou. boc mıabıt ſꝺ ɾꝛemıꞇ uıua

Monks and Minstrels

From around the 7th century AD, a style of music which is special to Western Europe began to appear.

Our earliest records of Western music come from the churches and monasteries of the Middle Ages. We know little about the popular music of this period, because musicians passed it from one to another without writing it down. But the medieval monks learnt to write down their music, using a system similar to the one used by modern musicians. With the help of this system, we can work out how the church music of the Middle Ages must have sounded.

Monks and Missionaries

The story of Western music begins with the early Christians who lived in the Middle East. An important part of their doctrine was 'spreading the word', and from Palestine, Christianity swept through the Greek and Roman empires and those countries which bordered the eastern part of the Mediterranean Sea.

As the power of the Roman Empire began to weaken in around the 3rd and 4th centuries AD, its armies retreated back to Italy and the 'Dark Ages' began. The Dark Ages lasted for hundreds of years, and the task of bringing the light to Western Europe fell to the Christian missionaries. Often

Below: Although only church music was written down during the Middle Ages, the paintings of the time show that a lively folk tradition also existed.

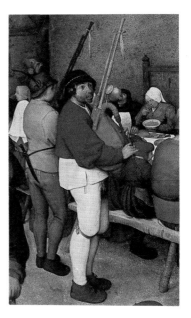

travelling alone, these monks visited the remotest parts of Western Europe, preaching throughout Britain, France and the Scandinavian countries. Wherever they went, they introduced people to their psalms and hymns.

The Dark Ages were a period of ignorance and superstition. Princes and peasants alike believed in magic and the forces of evil. It was thought best to keep on good terms with the local priest — even if this meant going to church several times a day. The spiritual advisers to the kings and their nobles played a powerful role, and as Christianity spread, the influence of priests and bishops grew. In monasteries, abbeys and cathedrals, learning and art flourished along with prayer.

Church Music

Most church music was a type of unaccompanied chanting called **plainsong**. Church organs were occasionally used, but other instruments were frowned upon by the church.

The most important part of the Christian service is

sing at eight services a day — the first long before dawn, and the last at nightfall.

Writing Music Down

The amount of music which the choirboys were expected to learn was amazing. On each of the many feast days the plainsong chants would be altered to commemorate a particular saint or festival.

To make memorizing the chants less difficult, signs called neumes were written over the Latin words of the chants. These helped the singer to remember the rough shape of the melody, but were no use in learning a new chant.

Above: Christian monks were largely responsible for the early development of western music.

the mass. As the Middle Ages progressed, church congregations took a less active part in singing and speaking the mass. Their contributions became limited to a few 'amens', while most of the singing was done by choirs of boys and monks.

The choirboys were really apprentice monks. They lived in the monasteries, and apart from their studies and domestic chores they had to

Above: An early example of written music.

Wandering Minstrels

The pious chanting of the monks was by no means the only type of music to be heard during the Middle Ages. Outside the church, folk dances varied from country to country, and even from one village to the next. It is thought that this type of music has changed little in the last 700 years.

Jongleurs and Troubadours

By the 11th century, much of Europe was in the hands of kings who ruled the land through their noblemen and princes.

Merchants and skilled craftsmen made up the middle class, to which belonged the jongleurs. These were minstrels who roamed the countryside in search of a patron willing to pay for their services.

A successful jongleur would join the household of a rich nobleman, and travel with him wherever he went. Apart from being skilled on a variety of instruments he would need to be a singer,

Left: Jongleurs would be expected to provide a whole evening's worth of entertainment.

juggler, acrobat and even an animal trainer.

Blondel de Nesle was the jongleur of King Richard the Lionheart, who was captured and imprisoned while returning from the Crusades. According to legend, Blondel searched the castles of Europe until one day he heard the king singing a song of his own composition. Having found the king, Blondel was able to hasten his return to England.

It was not unusual that King Richard was an accomplished poet, composer and performer, since such skills were considered to be a sign of education and refinement. These poet-musicians of noble birth were known as troubadours.

The knightly virtues of honour, bravery and courtliness were prominent in the poetry of the troubadours, especially when it concerned love. In the eyes of the courtly lover, his lady was pure and almost unobtainable. To be worthy of her gracious mercy, he had to prove his devotion with deeds of valour. In fact, there was a close link between the troubadour love songs and religious music in praise of the Virgin Mary. Sometimes the sacred **text** was simply replaced by a courtly poem.

Although some non-religious music written before the 12th century has been preserved, historical discoveries are more frequent from that time onwards. Much of the poetry and music written by the troubadours has been translated into modern musical language, and can be performed again today.

Below: A musician of the Middle Ages would have to be prepared to travel.

Lute

Medieval Instruments

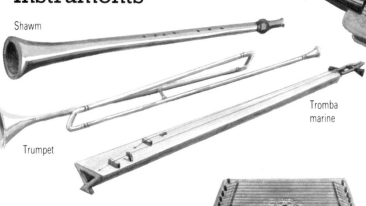

Shawm

Trumpet

Tromba marine

Psaltery

Throughout the Middle Ages, the use of instruments in church music became more common. As in the music of the troubadours, their role was almost always to accompany the voice.

Amongst the most favoured instruments were the bagpipes and the hurdy-gurdy — a stringed instrument which produced a similar sound to the bagpipes. Shaped like a sawn-off guitar with a handle at one end, the hurdy-gurdy's strings passed over a wooden wheel. With one hand the player turned the handle, which made the wheel scrape against the strings like a violin bow. With the other hand he pressed wooden keys against the strings to alter the notes.

A type of organ had been used in Jewish worship since long before Christ, and its use grew with the spread of Christianity. By the 13th century, some cathedrals had massive, cumbersome organs that needed several players. The mechanisms were so heavy that players needed to use their fists to push down the huge keys. Working the bellows to pump air into the organs was hard labour, and the sound produced was thunderous.

Fiddle

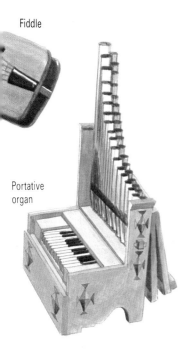

Hurdy-gurdy

Portative organ

The tiny portative organ, used both in sacred and secular (non-religious) music sounded more like a recorder. Only one hand was used to play the keyboard, while the other operated a small bellows.

Of all the many flutes and whistles to be found in medieval Europe, the recorder was the most versatile. There was also a three-holed pipe with nearly as wide a **range**. This pipe was always played with one hand, so that the player could also

accompany himself on the tabor (a type of drum). Drums were used on ceremonial occasions along with metal, horn or wooden trumpets. Though limited to two or three notes, these could only be matched in volume by the shawm — an ancestor of the modern oboe.

Stringed instruments were plentiful. Small harps, lyres, the round-bellied lute and psalteries were plucked with the fingers, while sticks were used to strike the strings of the dulcimer. The tromba marine, with its rather unearthly, rattling tone was perhaps the most unusual of the stringed instruments played with a bow, while the fiddle was amongst the most common.

Centres of Learning

During the Middle Ages, anyone wishing to become a scholar, or even to learn to read, would have to find a priest to teach them.

Important teachers tended to gather together, often in cathedrals or large monastic communities. It was here, particularly in the Notre Dame School in Paris, that musical ideas developed.

Breaking New Ground
Early Christian plainsong consisted of a simple tune which followed the rhythm of the words. Any instrumental **accompaniment** would simply copy or slightly decorate the **melody**, so that only one note sounded at a time.

During the Middle Ages, Western music became **harmonic**, with two or more different notes sounding together. It is the development of harmony which has made Western music unique (see also page 70).

The simplest kind of harmony occurs when one note, called a **drone**, is sounded continuously beneath the melody. The drone note stays still while the melody moves up and down. In the

Middle East, the use of the drone dates back thousands of years, and it was widely used in medieval popular music.

Harmony really began to develop around the 9th century with a technique in musical composition called **organum**. In its simplest form, a church choir was divided into two **parts**. The lower voices copied the movements of the upper voices, but always kept four or five notes below it. The two parts therefore moved in parallel with one another.

In the next stage of harmonic development, the two parts could move towards, away from or in parallel

to each other, while keeping either four, five or eight notes apart.

Above: Students would travel all over Europe to study with the teacher of their choice.

Music for Many Voices

From about the 13th century onwards, a new **polyphonic** style of composition appeared. Each part had its own melody and rhythm, even its own set of words: yet when all the parts were performed together they blended to make a musical whole. This early type of polyphonic composition was known as a **motet**, and although it used musical ideas that had come from the plainsong chants, it allowed composers far more creative freedom than plainsong. Towards the end of the Middle Ages, these new techniques were being used to write secular as well as sacred music.

Motets were too complicated to be learned by ear, so the choristers needed a more accurate form of notation. The old-fashioned neumes left too much to chance. In the 11th century, the Italian monk Guido of Arrezzo found that his choirboys learned their parts more easily if the notes were written across a series of horizontal lines, now called a **stave**.

The Renaissance

The period following the Middle Ages was a golden age of discovery and growth in Western Europe, with new ideas and attitudes affecting every area of life. Great technological advances led to the first round-the-world sea voyages, and, surprisingly, the world was discovered to be round instead of flat. New territories were conquered, and an attempt to find a new trading route to China and Japan resulted in the discovery of America and the west coast of Africa.

Fortunately, these developments in science, travel and politics were also accompanied by a flowering of art and learning. It is this re-birth, or 'renaissance' of knowledge that gives the period its name, and it was brought about by the rediscovery of the philosophy and science of the ancient Greeks. In treating music as a branch of science, the Greeks had used mathematics to measure and organize the notes and rhythms. Beginning in France and Italy during the 14th century, Renaissance composers began to introduce Greek theory into the writing of their music.

Whereas medieval scholars had looked to heaven for inspiration, their Renaissance counterparts turned to the lives of everyday people and the world around them. For the composers of music and poetry, this meant that the old knightly virtues of honour and chivalry proved to be less interesting than human passion and weakness. If you are able to listen to a recording of a 13th-century 'love' song, and then compare it with one written in the 15th or 16th century, the difference should be clear. Both words and music have become much more down-to-earth in the later period.

To make music more capable of expressing emotions, musicians needed to develop new techniques in composition. This also meant that instruments had to become more versatile, and this led to improvements and new inventions.

A Family of Instruments

Some medieval instruments, such as the hurdy-gurdy and the bagpipes, have survived as folk instruments up until modern times. But because they produce a steady drone, they were not suitable for playing the new polyphonic style of music.

Below: To demonstrate his power and splendour, the musical entourage of

Emperor Maximilian I of Germany accompanied him on all his state travels.

Below: The cornett, with its deepest-sounding relative, the serpent.

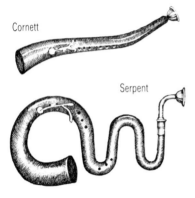

Cornett

Serpent

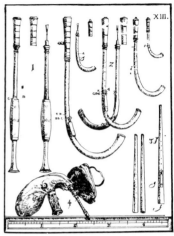

Above: Illustrations published in 1618, showing the scale of instruments

Other instruments from the Middle Ages continued to be used, but had to be improved to provide a wider range of notes. The effect of increasing the range was achieved by building 'families' — sets of different sizes of the same instrument. A group of instruments from the same family would sometimes play together as a consort, but most Renaissance music employed a 'broken', or mixed, consort.

Two instruments succeeded the medieval trumpet. The sackbut had a slide like a modern trombone, and was made from metal. The wooden cornett had a mouthpiece like a trumpet, but finger holes like a recorder. The largest relative of

the cornett was the serpent, which clearly takes its name from its curly shape.

During the Renaissance, the term 'flute' applied to recorders. The forerunner of the modern flute was called a 'German' flute, and was not thought to have as refined a tone as the recorder.

The dulcian, shawm, sordun and rackett all had a hollow reed which the player held in his mouth (like that of the oboe). The reed of the crumhorn, kortholt and cornamuse, however, was covered by a wooden cap through which the player would blow.

within their various 'families'. (Left: Shawms, crumhorns, cornetts and bagpipes; Centre: Members of the string family; Right: Drums.)

Although violins existed during the Renaissance, the most popular bowed instrument was the viol. This has a more restrained sound than the violin. The viol has six strings instead of the violin's four, the bow is gripped from below rather than above, and it is played resting on or between the knees.

Two families of instruments played by plucking at the strings were popular during this period. Those of the lute family had round, pear-shaped bodies and gut strings. Those related to the cittern had metal strings and a flat back.

The Renaissance also saw great advances in the building of keyboard instruments, organs in particular. Pressing down notes on the keyboard of a clavichord caused the strings to be struck, rather like a modern piano, while the strings of a harpsichord, spinet and virginal were plucked by the keyboard mechanism.

The division between loud instruments for ceremonial purposes and soft for private occasions was rigidly observed. The cornett was unusual in that it was the only instrument of the time to be played by both groups.

Change and Growth

The Renaissance upper classes regarded music as an essential social accomplishment, and the idea was not confined to the nobility alone. For people of all ranks, music occupied an important part in daily life, and one 16th-century traveller in Italy was amazed to find peasants playing the lute and shepherds reciting poetry.

Music at Court

With so many gifted amateurs, it might be supposed that the life of the professional musician would become increasingly difficult. However, music was also becoming more and more a symbol proclaiming power and wealth. Rival monarchs of the time tried to outshine each other in musical splendour. Francis I of France presided over a glittering court full of artists and musicians, while Henry VIII of England was himself a talented singer, composer and instrumentalist.

The most enviable position for the professional Renaissance musician was to be the valued musical servant of a prominent royal household. The highest post was usually organist or director of the royal chapel choir. His duties would include teaching as

Left: The tavern-like atmosphere of this 16th-century music college reflects the more down-to-earth attitudes of the Renaissance musician.

well as composing military, ceremonial, religious and dancing music.

Nobles of lower rank copied their king in musical rivalry with their neighbours, and any family of social standing would keep a variety of instruments available for guests and visitors.

This rivalry, linked with a genuine love of music, ensured that the Renaissance was a period of lively musical growth.

New Musical Ideas

During the Renaissance, musicians travelled all over Europe, exchanging styles and ideas wherever they went. Each country had its own style. The music of Italy, for example, tended to be warm and lively, while French and Flemish music was more dignified and restrained.

Many medieval forms of music were adapted to produce new effects. A medieval motet, for example, might have had four different texts (sets of words) being sung at the same time, each with its own contrasting rhythm and melodic shape. Renaissance composers changed this by using the same text for all four parts. This gave the music a feeling of unity. They then increased this effect by making the parts imitate each other. The same fragment of melody would be heard first in one part, then high up in the treble voices, then, a moment later, deep in the basses. At each new entry, the melody would weave in and out of its own echoes.

Below: The masque was a popular musical entertainment held at Renaissance courts.

The Madrigal

The new techniques were used for writing madrigals — a type of **part-song** for a small group of singers. These became a great favourite in the 16th and 17th centuries, especially in England.

Madrigal composers began to fit their music to the mood of the words in quite a new way. Madrigal poetry could be melancholy, rapturous, absurd or just plain bawdy; using a wide variety of rhythms and melodies, composers were able to use the music to heighten the emotions of the lyrics. A lament for a lost love might use long, slow notes to sound like a sigh, while a piece written to celebrate an official occasion might be lively, bright and stirring. Among the most important composers of madrigals were William Byrd, Thomas Morley, Orlando di Lasso and Giovanni Palestrina.

Many of the later madrigals were **homophonic** in style. Instead of the flowing and weaving of many independent voices in polyphony, the different parts in homophony move together to the main rhythm of the music. The result of this was that musicians became mainly concerned with the sound of the combined notes they were singing — an important development in Western harmony.

During this time, it became fashionable to sing only the highest part of a song. The lower voices could be replaced by instruments, such as a consort of viols, or a single lute.

Instruments Come Into Their Own

The early Renaissance was dominated by vocal music. Instruments were used mainly to accompany the

Below: A Renaissance 'broken consort'. This included instruments from more than one 'family'.

Right: Some sheet music was specially printed so that one page could be shared by players sitting around a table.

voice, or to play tunes for dancing.

However, by the end of the 16th century, the idea of listening to instruments for their own sake had led some composers to write completely instrumental works. One of the earliest forms of instrumental music was the **canzona**. This was a piece written in the style of a part song, but intended for instruments instead of voices.

Printing and Music

The growing number of musicians meant that there was an increasing demand for all types of music. Both church music and popular songs were rearranged for many different types and combinations of voices and instruments.

Without the discovery of the printing press in the mid-1400s, the demand for new pieces of music could not have been met. During the Middle Ages, only the most wealthy could afford books, as each one had to be laboriously copied out by hand. Now it became possible for people to buy printed music to play in their own homes.

The Baroque Era

During much of the 17th and 18th centuries, Europe was plagued by wars and political upheavals. In contrast, the orderly and elegant music of the period offered people a welcome escape from the chaos around them. Composers and performers, who were still grappling with the new ideas they had inherited from the Renaissance, had to develop even newer skills to create the splendour and brilliance demanded by their patrons.

Those with the money and power to shape musical fashion had become weary of the delicate, interweaving textures of the Renaissance. They had an appetite for music that was more spectacular and richly decorated. The term 'Baroque' was coined by critics of this music, who merely found it over-ornate and fussy.

The First Orchestras

The quiet and restrained instruments that were so dear to lovers of Renaissance music were not suitable for the forceful rhythms and virtuoso style of the Baroque. The lute fell from favour, while citterns and guitars became the instruments of amateurs only.

Viols were replaced by the members of the violin family, which sounded louder and brighter. These made up the greater part of the first orchestras, which had developed out of the court bands of the 17th century.

In addition to the strings, a Baroque orchestra might contain instruments such as

Left: A Baroque instrument maker.

the oboe, bassoon, flute or treble recorder, and, later, clarinet.

Unlike the modern orchestra, there would always be a harpsichord or an organ. New models were built which could produce enough sound to be heard while all the other instruments were playing. The harpsichord acquired a mechanism which enabled two or more strings to be plucked while the player pressed only one of the keys, and a similar idea was introduced into the building of organs. Pipes of different shapes provided the organist with a variety of contrasting sounds, and air could be sent to several pipes at once while depressing only one key.

The splendid Baroque pipe organ worked on air received from manually-operated bellows.

Monteverdi's *Orfeo* (1607).

Opera

The Baroque era in music is usually dated from the first **operas**, which were one of the most influential new ideas of the period. The beginnings of opera can be traced back to the **masques** and **pastorales** that became popular during the 16th century. These fashionable forms of dramatic entertainment used vocal and instrumental accompaniment, but the plot was unfolded by speech rather than song.

The first operas came about when a group of Italian poets and musicians sought to rediscover the simplicity and clarity of ancient Greek theatre. They invented a new singing style called **recitative**, which used a very simple accompaniment. The melody was made to follow the rhythms of ordinary speech; its function was to move the plot forward, but musically it lacked variety.

The great Italian composer, Monteverdi, is often called 'The Father of the Opera'. He relieved the monotony of long recitative passages with instrumental interludes and **arias** —long, elaborate songs for solo voice. In an aria, the words take second place to the music. A chorus of singers might also be used to provide further comment on the plot.

Ballet

The lavish masques of the Renaissance had featured displays of dancing, poetry and music. Whereas these had developed into opera in Italy, it was the dancing, or 'balleti', which caught the imagination of 17th-century France. Ballet flourished at the court of Louis XIV, where the 'Sun King' was himself an enthusiastic performer.

Early ballet used sumptuous costumes and scenery, but the restrained style of dancing was little more than a stately procession of gliding courtiers. In time, the steps became more lively and complex, and from being a leisurely pastime it developed into a skilled performing art for trained professionals.

Music at the French court was provided by composers such as Lully and Rameau, who wrote operas as well as ballets. The music of the new dances, such as the **gavotte**, the **bourré** and the **minuet** were to have far-reaching effects on instrumental music.

Right: King Louis XIV, dancing the role of the Sun.

Posts and Patronage

Handel

During the 17th and 18th centuries, composers were regarded in the same way as any other skilled craftsman. Street musicians could be hired by the hour, but anyone wishing to make a career in music had to obtain a regular post and work his way up. A composer might start out as a church organist in a small town and end up as the master of music to the king himself. A job in a humble municipal band could lead to one as an instrumentalist in the opera house.

Composers rarely wrote for their own pleasure. They were employed to meet the needs of their patron, whether it was the church, the state or the court. Monteverdi produced his opera *Orfeo* for the carnival celebrations at Mantua; Lully amused the French court with music for ballets, while in Germany, Bach was obliged to turn out a weekly **cantata** for the Sunday service at his church.

The career of George Frideric Handel spanned church, court and opera. Beginning as a church organist in Germany, he went on to make his name in Italy as an operatic composer and harpsichord virtuoso. He returned to Germany to take up the top musical post at the court of the Elector of Hanover, but by now his fame had spread. Handel deserted his post for greater glory in England — a move which caused him some embarrassment two years later, when the Elector of Hanover was made King of England.

As the popularity of opera began to decline in England, Handel began to write **oratorios**. These were rather like religious operas, but without any action or scenery — all the drama lay in the music itself. Handel's best-remembered oratorio is *The Messiah*.

Church Music

Dramatic religious music was encouraged by the leaders of both the Protestant and Catholic churches, who wished to attract larger congregations to their services. The greatest composer of this type of music was Johann Sebastian Bach.

Bach was partly influenced by the Protestant religious reformer Martin Luther, whose aim was to establish a church service in which all the congregation could take part. Previously, long services had been conducted in Latin, which ordinary people could not understand. Luther introduced chorales, or hymns, which could be sung easily by the congregation.

Bach lived a quiet and modest life in the service of the German church. The little fame he achieved during

The performance of a German church cantata.

his lifetime came from his reputation as an organ player. Today his works are seen as the perfect expression of the Baroque musical spirit, combining German logic with French delicacy and Italian passion.

Solo Performers

The popularity of the solo performer began with the first operas, where audiences were spellbound by the range and technical skill displayed by the singers. The vogue for virtuoso performances soon spread to instrumental music.

Although music still had strong links with the church at this time, its importance as a means of public entertainment was growing. The idea of a concert, where people would pay to listen to an instrumental performance, arrived in the late 17th century.

The **concerto** allowed an instrumental soloist to show off all his skill by carrying on a musical 'conversation' with an orchestra. In a concerto grosso, the single soloist would be replaced by two or more soloists.

A Change of Focus

Unlike the polyphonic music of the Renaissance period, in which all the separate parts were equally important, Baroque music gave more

Below: The delicate sound of the harpsichord made it ideal for solo pieces.

Above: A Baroque concert.

prominence to the upper and lower parts (the melody and the bass). The middle parts which lay in between these two took on a purely supporting role, and most composers of the period did not even bother to write them down. Instead, they wrote figures under the bass part, and from this 'figured bass' or 'basso continuo' a player could work out what to play in the middle parts.

The bass part itself was usually played by a bass viol or 'cello, while an organ or harpsichord player filled in the middle parts with his right hand and doubled the bass line with his left. This group of instrumentalists came to be known as the 'continuo', because they played throughout the piece. In a trio **sonata**, two instruments would play two melody lines, with a continuo accompaniment.

However, polyphonic music did not disappear with the arrival of the basso continuo. The device of passing a melodic idea from one part to another continued to be developed, especially in the keyboard music of such great German composers as Buxtehude and J.S. Bach. Their style of writing is known as **counterpoint**, and the greatest examples of this can be found in Bach's fugues.

Beauty and Balance

The word 'Classical' is often used to describe 'art' music, as opposed to popular music. More correctly it applies to the brief 60-year period from 1770 to 1830, when ideas in art, music and poetry were strongly influenced by the Classical cultures of ancient Rome and Greece. Since medieval times, Classical ideas have shaped artistic and scientific thinking, but each age has understood these ideals in a different way. Artists of the late Baroque found inspiration in the nymphs, cupids and playful gods of Classical mythology, but those of the late 18th century were more impressed by the formal beauty and noble simplicity of Classical architecture and sculpture. Similarly, whereas Baroque composers had sought to express emotional and dramatic ideas through music, their Classical counterparts created musical forms like sculptures in sound, whose beauty lay simply in the balance of the various parts.

C.P.E. Bach

Haydn

Below: The Pantheon, built in Paris during the 18th century, sums up the Classical ideal of beauty and elegance.

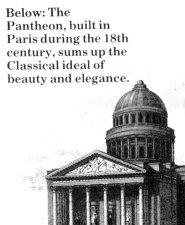
The Pantheon at Paris

One of Bach's sons, Carl Philipp Emanuel Bach, was an important musical link between the world of his father and the new Classical school. His music influenced many leading composers of the day, such as Haydn and Mozart, and helped to establish the forms that made the Classical era one of the most important periods in the growth of Western music.

Left: Chamber music was originally designed to be played at small, private gatherings, by a handful of musicians.

Getting Music into Shape

The desire to write longer, more interesting pieces of music had led medieval composers to lay a number of matching musical ideas end to end. This was then extended when, for example, the first musical idea was repeated again after each successive new idea.

Polyphonic composers made their ideas go further by the technique of passing the same musical fragment from one instrument or voice to another. Classical composers took this device and expanded the fragment into a fully-fledged musical idea, or theme. First the theme would be clearly stated, and then it would be developed. Its character would be transformed by altering the speed and rhythm of the melody, or the mood of the accompaniment; it would be broken up and mixed with different musical ideas; it was even played upside down and back to front. These themes and developments were the raw materials with which Classical composers built their perfectly-proportioned musical forms.

The Sonata

Drawing inspiration from the concerto grosso, operatic arias and sets, or 'suites' of dance tunes, composers such as C.P.E. Bach and Stamitz in Germany, and Corelli in Italy laid the foundations of the musical form which was to dominate the Classical period — the sonata.

A Classical sonata was made up of three or four 'movements'. These were separate pieces linked by a common musical idea. The first movement would be

Above: A Classical concert.

fast, the second one slow, and the third fast again. If there were four movements, a minuet or a **scherzo** would come between the second and third movements.

Each movement followed its own **form** or structure. The first movement would typically contain two main themes. Each would be played in succession, and then played for a second time. Next came the development of each theme, first separately and then in contrast. The movement would close with a further repetition of each theme in its original form.

Sonatas were written for solo piano or soloist plus piano, but they provided the basis for most types of Classical composition. A **symphony** is a sonata for an orchestra; a concerto uses the sonata form for a musical discussion between a soloist and the orchestra; a string quartet is a sonata for two violins, viola and 'cello.

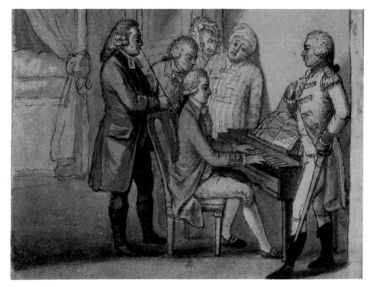

Mozart

One of the greatest composers of the Classical period was Wolfgang Amadeus Mozart, who was born in Salzburg in Austria in 1756. He was taken on his first concert tour at the age of six, performing before many of the leading rulers of Europe. Young Wolfgang returned home with a very considerable reputation and a taste for high living.

At the age of 12, Mozart was put in charge of the court orchestra in Salzburg. He was given leave to travel to Italy, where his work was greatly admired. By the age of 14, he had written two operas and many symphonies.

Mozart's employer at the court of Salzburg had been proud to have his gifted musician performing all over Europe, but his successor insisted that Mozart returned to Salzburg to carry out his obligations. After so much international fame, Mozart found his old job intolerable. After a heated argument, he was literally kicked out by his employer.

Mozart spent the last ten years of his life in Vienna, where he was to write his greatest music. However, despite success and recognition in his later years, Mozart died in poverty in 1791.

Beethoven

The fame of composers like Mozart had helped to make Vienna the musical capital of Europe, and it was there that the young Ludwig van Beethoven travelled to study under Hadyn in 1794. While his first compositions were inspired by the delicate music of Mozart and Haydn, Beethoven's fierce individuality soon made itself heard above the restrained Classical forms.

A new spirit of freedom was spreading across Europe in politics as well as in art. Beethoven was fired by the success of the French Revolution, and dedicated his Eroica symphony to Napoleon Bonaparte. However, when the Republican leader crowned himself Emperor of France, Beethoven tore up his dedication in scorn.

Beethoven was the first major composer to follow a musical career without having to rely on a post as a court musician. He was befriended by a number of rich aristocrats who supported him financially and encouraged him to develop his own musical ideas.

Towards the end of his life Beethoven became almost completely deaf. In spite of this, he continued to write and conduct some of his greatest work, until his death in 1827.

Beethoven

Beethoven's admiration for the young Bonaparte later turned to scorn.

The Age of Freedom

The writers, artists and musicians of the 19th century were greatly influenced by the 'Age of Revolution' which had swept across Europe at the end of the 18th century. As new democratic governments took away the ancient powers of royalty, ideals of personal and national liberty began to affect every area of life. The Romantic goal was freedom, together with a wish to achieve perfect harmony with Nature. In music, composers became less concerned with the importance of pure form for its own sake, and concentrated more on expressing their emotions, ideas and beliefs through their work.

The artistic seed from which Romanticism grew had in fact been planted long before this time. Almost all music contains some seeds of Romanticism, but while Classical composers had made sure it did not grow, the Romantics encouraged it to take over the entire garden. Beethoven was one of the first composers to introduce an 'emotional' element into his music, although he never allowed it to interfere with the structure of his compositions.

Franz Schubert, a contemporary of Beethoven's from Vienna, took this new mood even further.

While his symphonies possess a perfect Classical structure, the bulk of his work, particularly the songs (or lieder), were Romantic in nature. In these songs he achieved a balance between melody and accompaniment (usually voice and piano), which heightened the poetry of the text.

Musical Freedom

So that he should not have to waste time earning a living, Schubert's friends, none of whom were rich but who shared the same Romantic ideals, did their best to support him.

This was typical of a change of attitude that was taking place at the time towards art and artists, especially musicians. Up until the 19th century, music was usually written for a special purpose or occasion, after which it might never be played again. Romantic composers were only interested in music as a form of creative expression, and they would rather suffer poverty and hardship than sacrifice their artistic freedom. No longer a mere servant of the state, church or court, the musician had acquired an air of glamour.

Harpsichords and Pianos

Most Romantic composers wrote pieces for the piano, which replaced the harpsichord in popularity during the 19th century. The piano was a more versatile instrument, with a wide range and a powerful sound that was more in tune with the Romantic mood.

Composers such as Schubert, Chopin, Liszt, Brahms and Mendelssohn began to make use of the piano's special effects. They wrote short pieces with titles like Bagatelle, Nocturne, Prelude and Song Without Words, which were intended to evoke a certain mood, scene or idea.

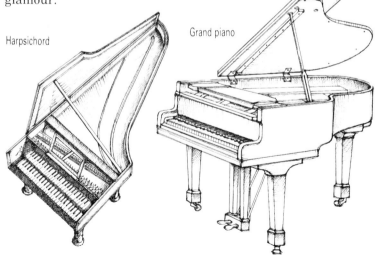

Harpsichord

Grand piano

The Power of the Orchestra

During the Romantic era, the symphony orchestra grew to allow a wider range of musical expression than ever before. The growth of the orchestra created the role of the conductor. Previously, one of the leading instrumentalists would have kept time, by waving a violin bow, for example. Now, however, it needed all of one person's attention, to control the speed and to bring out the expressive qualities of the music.

The basis of the 19th-century orchestra was still the string section of violins, violas, 'cellos and double basses, though in far greater numbers. To produce extra-deep notes, a huge double bass was built that needed one player to bow it and another, standing on a stool, to press down the strings.

The use of wind and percussion instruments had grown even more. Clarinets, flutes, oboes and bassoons made up the woodwind section, and instead of just one or two of each instrument, four or more were now used as well as the other members of their families. During this period, keys were fitted to woodwinds, and valves to horns and trumpets. This enabled their players to perform music which was more

symphonic form. Many preferred the freedom of the **symphonic poem** — an orchestral work intended to describe a particular scene, mood, personality or idea.

The technique of separating or blending the different instruments in an orchestra is known as **orchestration**. The various effects it produces can be described as **orchestral colour**, and Romantic composers used these colours to 'paint' pictures in sound.

Above: The Romantic orchestra

Below: Berlioz' enthusiasm for huge orchestras combined with brass bands and choirs was thought to be excessive by some of his contemporaries.

technically demanding. The brass section became a large and regular feature of the orchestra, with trumpets, trombones and tubas.

New instruments were invented to produce unusual sounds. The cor anglais, for example, made a more haunting noise than its cousin, the oboe. The new saxophone family produced a sound somewhere between the clarinet and the oboe.

Orchestral Paintings

The variety and range offered by the Romantic orchestra offered composers the chance to break away from the strictly Classical

Romantic Opera

Before the 19th century, Italian opera, with its arias, duets and dances separated by passages of spoken dialogue or recitative (sung narration) was so popular that composers of many nationalities wrote in the Italian style.

Italian operas were either Grand or Comic. Comic Opera was usually light and amusing; the music was easy to listen to and the plot generally ended happily for all concerned. The greatest Comic Operas were written by Mozart.

Composers of Grand Opera preferred subjects which were more serious and tragic. The plot was presented in a more flowing and continuous manner, without spoken dialogue. The melodies were still written in a popular style, but they were more melodramatic and had plenty of scope for the singers to show off their technical skills. The drama of the music was matched by exciting action and spectacular costumes and scenery.

The master of this style was Guiseppe Verdi, the son

of a poor Italian innkeeper. Verdi had to struggle hard for his living, but by his early thirties he was well on his way to international recognition as an operatic composer. *Aida* and *Rigoletto* are two of his operas which are still frequently performed.

Richard Wagner was born in 1813, the same year as Verdi. True to the Romantic spirit, Wagner's life, like much of his music, was stormy and passionate. Forever in debt and on the run from creditors or the police,

The thunderous, dramatic music of Wagner's *The Ring* uses a huge orchestra and chorus.

he dedicated himself to the fulfilment of a dream which he shared with many other Romantic thinkers — to combine music, poetry and drama into one art form. Wagner achieved this aim through his operas, by making the story and the way it was told as important as the music itself. He did away with the pattern of arias and recitative, and identified each of the characters with a distinctive musical theme (a leitmotif), which was played whenever they appeared in the plot.

Wagner

Verdi

Instrumental Fireworks

The 19th century was the great age of the instrumental superstar. The new freedom of expression in music allowed performers to display an unlimited range of emotions, and their passionate recitals made them the idols of the concert halls and the intimate **salons**.

When playing with an orchestral accompaniment, these virtuoso would perform works which had been deliberately composed to show off their technical brilliance, warmth and sensitivity. Stars like the Italian violinist Paganini toured the capital cities of Europe, where they would be greeted rapturously wherever they went.

In the salons, the pianist-composers Franz Liszt and Frederic Chopin drew groups of enthusiastic admirers — young women in particular. The poetic melancholy of Chopin was very different from the volcanic style of Liszt, but both moods satisfied the Romantic taste for emotional excess.

Below: The Romantic virtuoso was the idol of the salons.

Above: The life of Johann Strauss is told in the film *The Great Waltz* (1972).

Many other great Romantic composers began their musical careers as instrumentalists. Robert Schumann was so fanatical in his attempts to become a piano virtuoso that he used a mechanical device to widen the stretch of his hands. As a result, he injured his hand so badly that his career as a soloist was finished altogether, and he had to concentrate on composition.

Operettas and the Waltz

The political and industrial revolutions that took place in Europe at this time had created a new middle class. In general, this new group did not enjoy the work of the more 'highbrow' composers, but going to the opera and enjoying orchestral music was a sign of having 'arrived' socially. To meet the demand for a more popular style of orchestral music, composers such as Offenbach and Sullivan wrote **operettas**. These maintained the splendour of opera while matching the music and drama to the taste of the middle classes.

Another popular amusement for the rich were balls held in exclusive cafés and pleasure gardens. In Vienna, Johann Strauss led an orchestra which performed music especially for dancing. He wrote most of the music that the orchestra played, including such famous waltzes as *The Blue Danube*.

Nationalism

Towards the end of the 19th century, it seemed as if all the avenues of Romanticism had been fully explored. For almost 100 years, music had been dominated by German composers such as Beethoven, Wagner, and Johannes Brahms. Wagner was to the Romantic era what Bach and Beethoven had been to the Baroque and Classical periods; they simply left no room for development.

Italian and French composers such as Puccini and Fauré seemed content to carry on in the great traditions of their countries. It was left to Russia, Spain, Eastern Europe and Scandinavia to cultivate the new Nationalist movement.

To write music that was deliberately nationalistic was quite a revolutionary idea — up until this time composers of all nationalities had worked to make music an international language, understood by all. Naturally, composers had always been influenced to some extent by the traditional music of their own country. However, instead of trying to blend these influences into an international style, Nationalist composers exaggerated the importance of folk songs and dances in their music, choosing events from their country's history and daily life as subjects for operas and symphonic poems.

The first Nationalist opera was written by a Russian, Mikhail Glinka, in 1836. However, the movement did not get fully under way for another thirty years, at which time it turned Russia into a musical battlefield. This occurred when the champions of Russian Nationalism — Borodin, Mussorsky, Cui, Balakirev and Rimsky-Korsakov — attempted to discredit the work of Tchaikovsky. Tchaikovsky's music was

Above: The music of Edvard Grieg was inspired by the mountains and fjords of Norway.

Below: Traditional Russian folk musicians.

Grieg

unmistakably Russian in flavour, but he refused to be restricted by the limited musical language of his Nationalist countrymen.

Sibelius captured the feel of the lakes and forests of his native Finland in his symphonies. In Czechoslovakia, the Nationalist movement was founded by Smetana, carried on by Dvořák and taken into the 20th century by Janaček. In Spain, Albeniz, Falla and Granados filled their music with images of Moorish palaces and Flamenco dancers. Elgar flew the flag for England, while Charles Ives and Aaron Copeland helped to build the American Dream.

Into the 20th Century

Many composers who had grown up during the late 19th century attempted to re-kindle the spirit which had given birth to the music of Berlioz and Wagner. These were the Neo-Romantics (new Romantics), and they included Elgar, Holst, Sibelius, Mahler and Richard Strauss.

At the same time, some of their contemporaries were trying to lay the Romantic ghost. Tchaikovsky, Bruckner and César Franck followed Brahms' lead by fitting their music to the more formal structure of

Above: Mahler's conducting style was intense, emotional and dramatic.

Classical sonatas and symphonies.

At the start of the 20th century, these opposing ideas pulled the development of music in many different directions. Many artists went through periods during which they changed their musical style. Sibelius, for example, was at different times a Nationalist, a Neo-Romantic and an Impressionist. Increasingly, artists felt free to choose their own creative direction. As a result, it became harder to

Strauss' operas range from the dark and violent *Salomé* (left) to the elegant *Rosenkavalier*.

identify individual composers with any one musical tradition.

The Romantic Twilight

One of the composers who marked the end of the Romantic era was Gustav Mahler. A great admirer of Beethoven, Mahler's work was also inspired by the folk music and peasant dances of his native Austria. He had been sent to study piano in Vienna by his father, who had hoped that there was money to be made from having a famous performer for a son. Fortunately, his piano teacher recognized that Mahler's real talent lay in writing and conducting, and it was as a conductor that he first became famous on both sides of the Atlantic.

Since there was little money to be made out of composition, many composers had become orchestral conductors. Richard Strauss, for example, made his living this way, although he had been a published composer since the age of ten. Strauss became the conductor of the famous Berlin Philharmonic Orchestra, and established such a strong reputation that his career was able to survive a quarrel with Hitler's Nazi party.

Above: The young Béla Bartók collecting folk songs on a wax cylinder gramophone in 1918.

Meanwhile, the Nationalist movement had generated a new interest in folk music which had begun to die out as people moved from the country to the new industrial towns. For the first time, these traditional tunes were collected and studied in an academic manner. A number of 20th-century composers

67

helped in this important work, including Bartók and Kodály in Hungary and Vaughan-Williams in England. Because of this, traditional folk music came to play an important part in some of their compositions.

A Search for Originality

Developments in music have often been linked with those in the other arts, and when a new style of painting called Impressionism appeared during the late 19th century, it had a great effect on a group of composers living in France at that time. Impressionism aimed to make paintings more 'alive' by concentrating on the mood of a scene, rather than on its exact representation.

Claude Debussy aimed to do the same thing with music. By combining instruments in an original way, and developing a new style of harmonic writing, he produced a range of instrumental and orchestral effects which seemed to shimmer and glow with colour. *La Mer* is an orchestral work in which Debussy manages to depict the sea in many different moods and settings.

Maurice Ravel is another composer linked with this style of music, although his love of Classicism and strong rhythms never allowed him to be as lush and formless as Debussy.

It is perhaps rather sad that while Debussy intended to create an 'anti-Romantic' style, he is regarded by many modern musicians as the last of the great Romantic composers. It was left to his friend, Éric Satie to develop a style of writing which, being dry, witty and satirical, rejected once and for all the sugary-sweetness of Impressionism.

Left: A programme design for Debussy's ballet *L'Après Midi D'Un Faun*, which captures the shimmering stillness of a sun-drenched forest.

In their search for a new approach, a number of 20th-century composers began to blend forms and musical styles from pre-Romantic music with modern ideas of rhythm, harmony and instrumentation. This type of music is now called Neo-Classical. Its first composer was Busoni, an Austro-Italian who wrote several works in this style between 1897 and 1912. However, the movement really got under way with the work of the Russian composer Igor Stravinsky.

Like Satie and Ravel, Stravinsky was hired to write ballet music for the great Serge Diaghilev. Diaghilev's ability to spot exciting young talent had made him one of the most

Stravinsky was one of the most versatile composers of the 20th century. *Pulcinella* **(above) was written in the Neo-Classical style.**

influential figures in early 20th-century art, music and drama. In 1913, Stravinsky presented his ballet, *The Rite of Spring*, to a startled opening-night audience in Paris. The harsh sounds and unfamiliar rhythms caused an uproar in the theatre, and the effect it had can still be heard in music written today.

The Neo-Classical movement was carried on in Germany by Hindemith. A great admirer of the counterpoint of J.S. Bach, Hindemith's disciplined music sometimes has an almost machine-like precision.

Finding New Harmonies

Musicians use code words which help them talk to one another. However, no amount of words can convey the actual sound of music, and for that you must listen to the music itself.

What makes Western musical language unique is the use of harmony (two or more notes sounded together at the same time). **Example 1** shows the simplest form of harmony, which uses a 'drone'. The filled-in notes form the melody, and they are sounded as they are written — one after the other. The amount of time which passes after one melody note and the next is governed by the rhythm. The open notes form the drone acompaniment. This note is continually sounded, or in this case, regularly repeated, at the same time as the melody is played or sung.

Quite a lot of medieval music, especially dance music, required a drone accompaniment. Instruments such as the hurdy-gurdy or the bagpipes cannot be played without a drone.

The three following examples show, in a simplified way, how music became more versatile during the Middle Ages. **Example 2** shows two melodic lines which exactly follow each other's movements, both rhythmically and melodically. The distance between the upper and lower line (or part), always remains five notes apart.

Although the two melodies in **Example 3** have the same rhythm, they can move towards, away or in parallel to each other. They can share the same note (in **unison**), or are spaced four, five or eight notes apart.

The two parts in **Example 4** are rhythmically and melodically quite different. Because they move independently of each other, this example may be described as polyphonic.

By the end of the Middle Ages, polyphonic music for three or four parts was quite common, while Palestrina, one of the greatest Renaissance composers, wrote a mass for 40 parts.

Polyphonic music reached a creative peak through the genius of J.S. Bach, but Bach's intricate counterpoint was overshadowed by the new homophonic music,

Example 1

Example 2

Example 3

Example 4

where all the parts shared more or less the same rhythm. Both rhythm and harmony became more clearly defined, as musicians used them to shape and direct their music.

At all stages of harmonic development, the gravitational 'pull' of one note over the others led the listener's ear to understand the musical shape of the piece. A **key note** is the modern name for this effect, and once the relationship between this note and the melody has been established, the melody is said to be in a certain key. Since the Baroque period, musical progress has been closely connected with the way in which a piece of music has been able to break

away from the gravitational 'pull' of the key note.

Mozart and Beethoven used the close or distant relationships between different keys to construct Classical forms. The 19th-century composers were able to create emotional tension by pushing their music in unexpected directions, and not allowing it to fall back to its starting key. Late Romantic and Impressionist composers made increasing use of notes not belonging to the key, or even superimposed one key on top of another, to create an atmosphere of magic and mystery.

Musical Revolutionaries
Some 20th-century composers took this effect even

further. They decided that if they wanted to write music which sounded really modern, they would have to break away from the magnetic 'pull' of key altogether. This was not so easy to do. We are so used to hearing music which has a key note at its centre that even four notes, struck at random on a piano keyboard, are likely to give us a feeling of what notes to expect next, or that one note seems more important than another.

Despite various attempts to lessen the effect of the key, such as playing in two or more keys at once, or deliberately using a chord which clashes with the melody note, it seemed impossible to write music with no key at all.

Schoenberg and 12-Tone

In 1913, the Austrian composer Arnold Schoenberg devised a method of composition that finally broke the chains of key. In his 'serial' or '12-tone' music, the 12 notes from which all Western music is made up are treated as being exactly equal.

To compose this kind of music, the 12 notes are first arranged in any order the composer wishes, to make a musical theme. The arrangement of the notes in the theme is called a 'tone row' or 'series', and once the 'row' has been fixed the notes may only be sounded in that order. To produce varied musical effects, the row may then be played back to front or upside down, and may start on any of the notes.

Schoenberg's method meant that although the familiar pull of key had been removed, the music was still kept within a strong framework. However, like his pupil, Berg, he saw no reason why the rigorous discipline of 12-tone composition should not be combined

Left: Schoenberg wrote *Pierrot Lunaire* for a Berlin cabaret in 1912. He used a new vocal technique called 'Sprechgesang' (half-speech, half-song).

Varèse

The percussive music of Varèse echoes the harsh, metallic sounds of the industrial city.

with emotional and dramatic expressiveness.

But perhaps the most influential 20th-century composer will prove to be Anton Webern. Webern constructed 'rows' not only from notes but also from rhythms and other elements which go to shape music. His works are so concentrated and precise that Stravinsky described them as 'dazzling diamonds'.

Finding New Sounds

Meanwhile, two quite unconnected things had inspired other experimental composers to produce a harsh and aggressive style of music.

One was the industrial noise of modern cities and machinery, and the other was the discovery of the music of Africa and the Far East.

Edgar Varèse, a French composer living in America, combined the sounds of the street and the factory with the infinitely complex rhythms of primitive music. He rejected the musical language of 19th-century Romanticism, with its self-expression and lush orchestral sounds, and even turned his back on melody and harmony. Instead, his music gives the impression of great slabs of sound colliding with each other.

The American composer John Cage carried the musical revolt even further, abandoning not only musical structure but also in some cases sound itself. He strips music to its most basic ingredients — sound and no sound. Some of Cage's music contains long periods of silence, while in others he anticipated the invention of the synthesizer by using a 'prepared' piano. This involves putting nuts, bolts and bits of wood in the works of the piano so that it produces unusual sounds.

Cage also helped to pioneer the idea that part of the process of composition should be left to the performer. One of his works even includes the coughing and shuffling of the audience.

Tapes and Synthesizers

As composers learnt more about the science of music, they wanted to control every detail of the sound in a way which was beyond the ability of even the finest players. With the invention of the tape recorder and the synthesizer, the composer could have complete control over his music.

In France, Sheaffer, Messiaen and Boulez recorded non-musical sounds in city streets, factories and railway stations — sounds that conjured up the urban, industrial life of the modern age. By slowing the recording down, or playing it backwards and then mixing the sounds together, they created the abstract forms of *musique concrète*.

In 1959, the American recording company RCA built an electronic synthesizer that was capable of producing any sound imaginable. It was massive by today's standards, and instead of a keyboard, it received the composer's signals by means of two typewriters.

Above: The RCA synthesizer.

Below: Karlheinz Stockhausen.

The most important work in early electronic music was carried out in Germany by Karlheinz Stockhausen. At different times he uses vocal, instrumental, synthesized and taped sounds as the raw material from which he builds his compositions.

His music is constructed like a complex mathematical equation, with every single detail under control. Carrying on from Webern's work, he constructs 'rows' not only from notes and rhythms but from degrees of loudness or softness, from the way an instrument sounds or blends with others, or even how a sound begins and ends.

Popular Music

One of the great changes to take place during the 20th century has been the growth and development of popular music. Although a lighter kind of music has always existed outside the scholarly tradition of art music, we have little information about it apart from the fact that it existed. However, popular music today is a huge industry, catering for a wide variety of tastes and reaching its audiences not only through live performances and shows, but also through tapes, records, video, radio, film and TV. One of the reasons for this development in popular music was the social change that took place during the 19th century, when many people left their small country villages to find work in the towns. While the Nationalist movement was doing its best to preserve the great treasure store of folk music that had been ignored by music historians for so long, many of the local musicians who had kept this music alive now abandoned their traditional roots for a new way of life.

At the same time, the growing town population

Below: Classical violinist Yehudi Menuhin (left) and his jazz contemporary Stéphane Grappelli (right) have crossed the barriers of 'art' and 'popular' music by playing together on a number of occasions.

Right: The cheapest Music Hall seats were up in the gallery where the audience took a lively interest in the proceedings.

had found a new form of entertainment — the Music Hall, or Vaudeville. Beginning in public bars but later moving to specially-built theatres, this type of entertainment usually featured a wide variety of acts, such as dancers, acrobats, magicians and comedians. A Master of Ceremonies would introduce the artists, and try to keep the audience quiet. The star of the show was often a singer, and before records became widely available, people would buy printed copies of their songs to play at home.

Below: The Hollywood musical of the 1930s can be traced back to the Music Hall and operetta.

Up until the early part of this century, it was usual for almost everyone to sing and, if they could get hold of one, play a musical instrument. But as more people began to have enough time and money to go to the Music Hall or to operettas, a gradual change took place in popular music: instead of making music at home, people began to rely on professional performers to provide their entertainment for them. By the early 20th century, the arrival of the gramophone and radio had led to an even greater dependence on commercially-produced music.

Folk Music Today

It was left to an increasingly small number of people to keep alive the traditional songs and dance tunes that make up folk music.

If we could follow the path of folk music back through time, we would almost certainly find that it began with the magical rites of the prehistoric cavemen. The themes of many folk songs and dances are connected with the magic of birth, death, springtime or harvest, and while morris dancers perform for fun today, each team or 'side' still has its own jealously-guarded steps and tunes which may originally have had some magical importance.

At one time, the people living in remote country areas would scarcely be aware of the different musical traditions outside their own village. Now that radio can reach every corner of the world, some of this unique music is in danger of becoming extinct.

Although many enthusiasts work hard to preserve folk music, it is no longer performed in the home but in special clubs and concert halls. It is simple music, to reflect simple joys and sorrows. Perhaps the harsh and agressive sounds of Rock music reflect modern life more accurately.

Below: The Isle of Wight folk festival.

Back to the Roots

During the last years of the 19th century, a new type of music began to make itself heard in the southern states of the USA. These were the early sounds of Jazz, which developed into a style which reached its height of popularity in the 1930s and 1940s. Jazz has had a great influence on all kinds of popular and even classical music, and it shares its roots with one of the dominant forces in pop music today — Rock. These roots are found in the kind of music called 'the Blues'.

The story of the Blues begins as long ago as the 16th century, and as far afield as West Africa. It was from there that the first slaves were taken to work in the sugar and cotton plantations of the Caribbean and the USA.

As well as a means of entertainment, music had played an important part in many aspects of everyday African life, such as work, trade, courtship and religion, while drums were used to pass messages. On the American plantations, the white bosses began to realize that drum messages were helping slaves to escape, and so they banned their use. However, the slaves continued to sing work-songs to ease their labour. The work leader would sing a line, and the others would reply with a repeated chorus.

Calypso and Reggae

Slavery was abolished in America in 1865. While some ex-slaves returned to Africa, others settled in the Caribbean or the southern states of the USA.

The music of those who stayed in the Caribbean was influenced by music from Cuba, Brazil, Mexico and other Latin American countries. A type of song called 'Calypso' resulted from the blend of African drumming, Latin American guitars and whistles, and a newly-invented Caribbean instrument — the steel pan.

In the 1960s, radio brought American Soul and Rock music to the ears of Caribbean musicians. With the introduction of the electric guitar, a style of music called Reggae appeared. By the beginning of the 1980s, many white bands were imitating the Reggae beat of bands such as Bob Marley and the Wailers.

The influence of such early Blues singers as Big Bill Broonzy (left) can be heard in Gospel music (below).

The Birth of the Blues

The Blues probably grew out of plantation work songs and laments. As a song form, the second line is a repeat of the first, while the third usually comments on the first two. In its most simple form, the melody is repeated three times with a different harmonic accompaniment for each line. This musical pattern still forms the basis for many Rock tunes.

There is also a distinct style of Blues singing which has had an even greater effect on modern pop music. This rich and plaintive vocal style soon found its way into the church. At first, these religious songs, which were

Above: The marching bands played funeral dirges as well as dance tunes.

called spirituals, were sung by an unaccompanied choir, but later on an electric organ, bass and drums were added. Eventually, the music developed a more rhythmic style, which became known as 'Gospel'.

In the meantime, some of the freed slaves formed brass bands which played marches in the street. On long parades, the bands would become bored with playing the same tunes over and over again, and so they began to 'improvise' — to make up their parts as they went along.

81

and into the nightclubs and bars, it was necessary to invent a drum 'kit' that could be played by a single player. The move indoors also meant that non-portable instruments such as piano and double bass could be added to the band's line-up.

Jazz was the product of many traditions. As well as the Blues and the marching bands, the pulsing sound of Ragtime began to be heard in the music. Its two greatest composers were Scott Joplin and Eubie Blake, who wrote Rags to be played on the piano. However, as Jazz pianists like 'Jelly Roll' Morton began to incorporate the jerky, rhythmical style into their playing, other members of the band began to copy it.

The same musicians who played in the marching bands in the daytime began to work in the saloons and gambling dives at night. A rhythm section (perhaps a guitar or banjo, tuba and drums) would repeat the accompaniment over and over again, while the soloists (on trombone, trumpet, clarinet or saxophone) played the tune and took it in turns to improvise.

Early Jazz bands used only those instruments that could be carried in a parade. However, a marching band used at least three drummers, for the bass drum, side drum and cymbals. Once Jazz moved off the streets

Big Bands to Be-Bop

Early Jazz was played almost exclusively by black musicians, but as it became fashionable, more white Jazz bands appeared. From being the music of the poor, it became the craze of the wealthy. The new customers could afford to hire more musicians, and so Jazz bands grew into the thirty- or forty-strong big bands of the 1930s and 1940s.

Apart from piano, guitar, double bass and drums, the big bands contained mainly trumpet, trombone and saxophone players, who might also play clarinet and flute. Big band leaders like Glenn Miller and Benny Goodman became international celebrities, and helped to turn Jazz into big business for the first time.

During the '30s and '40s, many of the greatest names in Jazz played as 'side-men' in these bands. The same players formed smaller groups, who played in all-night clubs after their big band set had finished. John Coltrane, Charlie Parker, Theolonius

Scott Joplin

Monk and Dizzy Gillespie are just a few of the musicians who created a new style of Jazz called 'Be-bop', which restored the important role of improvisation to Jazz. Later, band leaders like Count Basie and Earl Hines adapted Be-bop to the big band sound.

Below: The Original Dixieland Jazz Band.

Back to the Blues

Although white players have adopted Jazz, the greatest names in Jazz have always belonged to black musicians. To understand this, it is worth remembering that the Blues, the root of all Jazz, was not only a musical form but also the expression of anger and despair in the face of oppression.

Boogie-woogie is a kind of Blues played on the piano. It has a driving, pounding rhythm, with eight instead of the more usual four beats to the bar. Sometimes the eight beats are evenly spaced, giving the chugging effect of a steam locomotive, while at other times the music hammers away to a more uneven rhythm.

When this piano style was combined with the guitar and vocal style of the Blues and reinforced with bass and drums, a new style of music called Rhythm and Blues emerged. 'R 'n B' was helped along by the invention of the electric guitar, which had been produced to enable the guitar and double bass to be heard while playing with a large Jazz band. The new electric guitar and bass gave R 'n B an added force and drive, which can be heard in the music of Fats Domino and Little Richard.

Below: The Little Richard Band.

The growth of popular music has been a complicated process. The chart above gives a very simplified account of the development of the Blues to Rock'n Roll.

Rock'n Roll

Although R 'n B produced some of the earliest and greatest Rock stars, some years passed before their music became commercially successful, either in Europe or the greater part of America. When it did, it was performed by white Americans such as Bill Haley and Elvis Presley and it became known as 'Rock 'n Roll'.

As well as R 'n B, Rock 'n Roll contains elements of Country and Western music. Both the words and music of Country songs are plain and simple, reflecting the attitudes of farmers and small-town dwellers in the southern and mid-western states of America.

Rock 'n Roll was quickly taken up by a generation of teenagers who were eager to replace the old-fashioned values of their parents. Although the original raw energies of the music have often become sacrificed for the sake of commercial success, Rock has always managed to re-emerge in one form or another as the mouthpiece of yet another generation.

For some time, Rock 'n Roll was dominated by American stars such as Buddy Holly and the Everley Brothers, whose songs mainly reflected the sentimental influence of Country music.

Below: Rock'n Roll got the audiences back onto the dance floor.

However, in the 1960s a number of British bands like the Rolling Stones began to play their home-grown version of the more aggressive R 'n B. It was at this time that the Beatles set out on a career that was to revolutionize pop music.

Before the Beatles came along, it was not usual for an established singer or group to alter their musical style unless they were forced to move with the musical fashion. However, the Beatles continued to experiment with new ideas and created their own fashions — not only in music, but in dress and social behaviour. Their fame quickly spread from Britain to America, until the whole world succumbed to 'Beatlemania'.

Above: An outbreak of Beatlemania at London airport in 1966.

By the early 1970s, Rock music had become concerned with ideas of freedom, peace, brotherhood and love. Singer-songwriters like Bob Dylan wrote protest songs about social injustice, while others staged concerts to raise money for the starving third world countries.

In the meantime, black Rock music was growing independently. With some help from Jazz and Gospel, it developed into a style called 'Soul'. Ray Charles was one of the earliest Soul musicians, while Aretha Franklin, Diana Ross and Stevie Wonder helped to bring it into the '70s and '80s.

Into the '80s

During the 1960s, the Beatles showed that it was possible for successful musicians to break away from the control of backers and record companies. They became successful enough to control their own finances, and to record music for its own sake rather than to meet the demands of the current fashion. As a result, other musicians in the late '60s and early '70s were encouraged to try out new ideas, which might not have been considered in a more strictly commercial atmosphere.

The many experiments in musical styles and recording techniques which took place helped to pave the way for the experimental attitude of the 1980s. A glance at today's album or singles charts will reveal a wide variety of styles, from Heavy Metal to Electro-pop. Many outside influences have recently been absorbed into pop music. 'Disco' began a new dance craze with its blend of Jazz, Soul and Rock, while the Reggae music of bands such as Bob Marley and the Wailers has had an enormous influence.

Up until the mid-1970s, only a few Rock artists attempted to make their act theatrical. Many preferred not to put on a show at all, but let the music speak for itself. This began to change when certain performers began to act out parts of their songs, and the idea grew until artists like David Bowie adopted a role which was maintained throughout a whole series of concerts. Complete Rock operas, such as *Tommy* by the Who, appeared. By the end of the 1970s, no Rock concert was complete without its light show and special effects.

The Punk movement was an attempt to strip away

Left: Reggae superstar Bob Marley

Above: The changing image of David Bowie.

all the glitter that had come to surround Rock music, so that it could re-emerge once again as the expression of anger and rebellion. However, most of the Punk bands eventually became toned down by commercial success.

The rapidly-changing fashions of modern pop music has led many bands to enjoy a brief blaze of glory followed by complete oblivion. Honourable exceptions include artists like Bowie, whose success lies in his ability to keep one step ahead of current musical trends.

Pop and Technology

Recent technological inventions have made all sorts of new effects possible for musicians today, but some would argue that the losses are greater than the gains. Video recordings, for example, have brought a new slick theatricality to Rock, but videos lack the spontanaeity of live performances.

Increasingly, all kinds of commercial music has had more to do with computer programmers than with musicians, since one string synthesizer player is cheaper than twenty violinists. This is the age of the chip, but hopefully, when we are all thoroughly bored with machine music, we will rediscover the pleasure of making our own music.

Glossary

Accompaniment A musical background to the melody.

Aria An operatic song.

Bourée A 17th-century dance with a fast, driving rhythm.

Cantata A musical drama, like an opera but without acting, scenery or costume.

Canzona Originally a type of Italian poetry, spoken or in song form; an instrumental version of such a song.

Concerto An instrumental composition in which the playing of one or more soloist is contrasted with the playing of the whole orchestra.

Counterpoint A term used to describe the development of polyphonic music during the Baroque period.

Drone The simplest form of harmonic accompaniment to a melody, in which one note is repeatedly sounded.

Form The overall shape of a piece of music.

Gavotte A country dance which became fashionable during the 17th century.

Harmony When two or more notes are sounded simultaneously.

Homophony Music in which all the parts keep to the same harmony and rhythm.

Key note On hearing almost any fragment of melody, the human ear searches for one note which will act like a centre of gravity for the other notes in the melody. The modern word for this gravitational pull is 'tonality', and the centre note is the 'key note'.

Masque A dramatic entertainment with musical accompaniment, popular with the nobility during the 16th and 17th centuries.

Melody When single notes follow one another to form a progression of higher or lower notes.

Minuet A French country dance, which found a place in art music from the late Renaissance onwards.

Motet A type of polyphonic composition, originally used in medieval church music.

Notation The system used for writing music down.

Opera A dramatic production involving vocal and orchestral music, in which the characters sing rather than speak their lines.

Operetta This retains the spectacle of opera, but the music and the subject matter are usually less serious.

Oratorio Similar to a cantata, but with a religious text.

Orchestral colour Every voice or instrument has its

own sound or 'tone colour', and each different combination of orchestral instruments has a distinctive 'orchestral colour'.

Orchestration The art of combining orchestral instruments to produce a particular effect.

Organum Harmonized version of plainsong chants; the earliest form of polyphony.

Part Where two or more melodies are sounded simultaneously to make a harmonic composition, each melodic line is called a 'part'.

Part-song A vocal composition for two or more voices.

Pastorale A 16th-century musical dramatic performance.

Plainsong Early Christian church music, sung in unison and following the natural rhythm of the words.

Polyphony Music with several independently moving parts, each with their own rhythmic and melodic lines.

Range The distance between the highest and lowest notes which a voice or instrument can produce, or the upper and lower limits of a melody.

Recitative An operatic style of singing which allows the natural rhythm of the words to shape the melody.

Rhythm The beat or pulse of a piece of music.

Salon A private room used for concerts.

Scherzo A faster, livelier version of the minuet.

Sonata A Classical sonata is normally made up of four separate pieces, called 'movements'. The first movement is usually fast, the second slow, the third a minuet or scherzo and the fourth fast again. During the Baroque era, the sonata's structure was similar to that of the orchestral dance suite, which meant it had more movements.

Stave A system of horizontal lines used to write down music. The position of a note on the stave tells a musician which note to play or sing.

Symphonic poem An orchestral composition equal in size and seriousness to a Classical symphony, but emphasizing musical feeling rather than form.

Symphony An orchestral work, sharing the same framework as the sonata.

Text The words used in a piece of vocal music.

Unison Produced when the same note is sounded simultaneously by more than one instrument or voice.

Virtuoso A performer who achieves musical excellence.

Index

Page numbers in *italics* refer to illustrations.

Acknowledgements

Photographs:
Pages: 2/3 De Monde Advertising, 4 Fotomas, 6/7 & 11 David Redfern, 12 National Film Archive, 13 Popperfoto, 17, 22/23 & 24 Michael Holford, 25 Kunsthistorisches Museum, Austria, 27 Bodleian Library, 34, 35 & 41 Fotomas, 42 Bildarchiv Preussischer Kulturbesitz, 48 Wallace Collection, 49, 51 Mansell Collection, 52/53 Mary Evans Picture Library, 54 Salzburger Museum, 56 Staatliche Kunstammlungen, 59 Fotomas, 63 National Film Archive, 65 Zefa, 67 G.D. Hackett Photography, 68 E.T. Archives, 73 Syndication International, 75 Hulton Picture Library, 74/75 RCA, New York, 76 (left) Clive Barda, 76 (right) Hulton Picture Library, 77 National Film Archive, 78 David Redfern, 80, 81, 83 & 84 Frank Driggs Collection, 87 Keystone Press Agency, 88, 89 David Redfern.

Picture Research: Penny Warn.

Artwork:
Mark Bergin, John James (Temple Art), Peter Gregory. Front cover: Roger Payne